QUESTIONS AND ANSWERS ABOUT HORSES

by **MILLICENT E. SELSAM** illustrated by **SANDY RABINOWITZ**

SCHOLASTIC INC.

New York Toronto London Auckl...

CONTENTS

A horse walks on the tip of its toes. There is one toe on each foot. Each toe is covered with a hoof that protects it as the horse runs over the rough ground.

Because a horse has long legs, it can run very fast. The horse is always ready to run if anything scares it.

Today almost all horses are domesticated. That means they are taken care of by people who give them a place to live and food to eat.

Do all horses look alike?

No. There are about 60 different kinds of horses. All the different kinds we have today have been developed by people who wanted fast horses, or strong horses, or horses that jumped well for horse shows, or gentle little horses for children to ride. To get the kinds they wanted, they mated horses that had these qualities.

Suppose someone wanted to raise horses that could run very very fast. He would mate two fast horses. Then he would watch their baby horses as they grew up. He would pick the two fastest of those young horses and mate *them*. When this picking or *selecting* is done for a few generations, you are likely to get the kind of very fast horse you want.

People who select and mate horses to develop horses with special qualities — speed, or strength, or size — are called *horse breeders*.

What are some special breeds of horses?

THE THOROUGHBRED

The Thoroughbred is a fast-running race horse. It can run 40 miles an hour for a short distance. (Most racetracks are about a mile long.) This breed began in England when three male horses (stallions) from Africa and Arabia were mated to English female horses (mares). That was more than 250 years ago.

THE SHETLAND PONY

The Shetland Pony comes from the Shetland Islands, 100 miles northeast of Scotland. The land there is rocky and bare. There is not much grass growing on the islands. Bigger horses weren't able to get enough grass to eat, so they all died out.

But the smaller horses did not need so much grass. They were able to grow up and have young ones who were also small like their parents.

And that is how, over the years, the breed of small Shetland ponies developed.

THE AMERICAN SADDLE HORSE

The American Saddle Horse is one of the most popular riding horses. It has a smooth way of walking and running. It was bred in pioneer times in the days when people needed comfortable horses to ride on bad roads and across country lanes and fields.

THE QUARTER HORSE

The Quarter Horse was the first horse bred by the pioneers in the New World. It was named the *Quarter Horse* because it was good at racing a quarter-mile distance. But it could also work long hours without getting tired.

Today the Quarter Horse is a popular all-around work horse in the West. Cowboys use it on ranches to round up cattle, rope calves for branding, and separate cows from the herd. It is also used for riding rugged western trails.

THE DRAFT HORSE

The Draft Horse is a large, strong horse used for drawing heavy loads on farms. It was much used in the days before tractors. But you can find the Draft Horse wherever farmers are still using horses to work their land.

One kind of Draft Horse called the *Percheron* weighs about a ton — 2,000 pounds. These horses are so steady and dependable that they are used in circuses. The performers ride bareback, stand, and sometimes do somersaults on the Percherons' broad backs.

The *Clydesdale,* a very handsome Draft Horse, is often used to pull wagons in parades.

The ancestors of Draft Horses were the warhorses of the Middle Ages. They carried knights in heavy armor.

THE ARABIAN HORSE

The Arabs of desert Arabia bred this horse hundreds of years ago. It is the oldest and purest breed.

The Arabian Horse is fast and strong. When people want other types of horses to be faster and stronger, they mate them with Arabian horses. They hope that the colts born will be as fast and strong as the Arabian parent.

THE WESTERN MUSTANG

This is the tough small horse of the wild West. Like the Quarter Horse it is used for rounding up cattle. It was once the favorite horse for the Pony Express. It could gallop over rough, rocky land for many hours.

The mustangs are the descendants of the horses brought to America by the Spaniards more than 400 years ago.

THE LIPPIZAN HORSE

This breed of beautiful white horses was developed in Austria about 400 years ago. They were bred mostly from horses imported from Spain and Italy.

The Lippizan horses are trained at the Spanish riding school in Vienna, Austria. They learn to do difficult exercises and dance movements to music.

When they are born, Lippizans are a very dark color. Gradually they get lighter and lighter. By the time the horses are ten years old, they are snow white.

Are there any really wild horses still left anywhere?

The only really wild horse in the world is the Prze-walski (**shi-val-skee**) horse. Thousands of years ago wild herds of this horse roamed over the grasslands of Asia and Europe. But by 1970, there were fewer than 1,000 Przewalski horses alive, and all of them were in zoos and game reserves.

Then, in 1994, twenty Przewalski horses from a reserve in the Netherlands were taken to Mongolia in Asia — the place where the breed had died out in the 1960s. Scientists hope the horses will learn to live again on the plains of Mongolia, just as they did before. The chances look good. Several foals have already been born.

Does the horse have any relatives alive in the world today?

Yes. Wild asses, donkeys, and zebras are the horse's relatives.

Wild asses live in Asia and Africa, and may have a few shoulder stripes.

Zebras live only in Africa and have many stripes.

WILD ASS

ZEBRA

Donkeys are asses that have been domesticated and bred with each other for many years. There is a special kind of small donkey called a *burro*. It is used mainly as a pack animal in the southwest of the United States, in Mexico, and in Spain.

When a mother horse and a father donkey are mated with each other, the baby that is born is a *mule*. A mule can never have offspring.

DONKEY

BURRO

How long does a baby horse have to grow inside its mother before it is born?

It grows inside its mother for about 11 months. A foal (baby horse) can stand and run within an hour or two after it is born. It gets milk from its mother. About a week after it is born it begins to nibble on grasses, too.

How long does it take for a horse to grow up?

A horse is half grown when it is one year old. It takes five years to be fully grown.

How long does a horse live?

Most horses live about 20 years. But some horses have lived to be 40 to 50 years old.

What does a horse eat?

A horse eats grass, hay, and grain. The grain is usually oats. But the oats are sometimes mixed with corn,

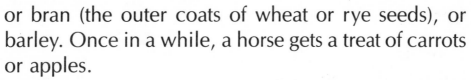

or bran (the outer coats of wheat or rye seeds), or barley. Once in a while, a horse gets a treat of carrots or apples.

When a horse grazes in the field, it covers a lot of ground. It takes a mouthful or two of grass and then moves a step. Then it eats another mouthful and moves on.

If a horse is not grazing outside, it is fed grain and hay two or three times a day.

How much does a horse cost?

A horse costs anything from $100 to over one million dollars.

How much does it cost to keep a horse?

If you have a barn to keep him in, the food alone would probably cost about $100 a month.

What else does a horse need besides food?

A horse needs water. It drinks between 12 and 20 gallons of water a day.

A horse also needs grooming — which means it has to be brushed and wiped to remove dirt and sweat.

A horse needs shoes.

Once or twice a year a horse has to be checked by a veterinarian. It needs to be vaccinated against diseases, such as tetanus. Sometimes it needs to have its teeth filed down to remove sharp edges.

A horse also needs exercise.

A horse needs someone who has time to take good care of it.

How much does a horse weigh?

Most horses weigh between 900 and 1200 pounds. But it depends on the kind of horse you are talking about. Some draft horses weigh over a ton.

How does a horse sleep?

Sometimes a horse sleeps standing up. Sometimes it lies down to sleep. It usually takes short naps in the daytime. But at night it may sleep a few hours at a time.

Can a horse see very well?

The horse can see in front and behind at the same time because its eyes are on the sides of its head. A horse can notice the smallest movement. It can see danger coming, even while it is eating grass.

Its eyes are protected by long eyelashes that help to keep the dust out.

Does a horse use its tail for anything?

A horse uses its tail to keep flies and other insects away. Sometimes horses stand alongside each other with the tail of one next to the head of the other. In this way, each one helps to keep flies off the other.

Can a horse find its way home to its stable?

When a horse knows the neighborhood it is in, it can find its way home easily, just as you would. It uses landmarks — places it has come to recognize — as a guide.

A horse can also use its sense of smell if the wind is blowing from the direction of the stables. The horse just keeps walking or running into the wind. The smell gets stronger and stronger as the horse gets nearer home.

What happens when two horses meet for the first time?

First they circle around each other. Then they touch noses. After that each horse smells and touches the other's body and tail with the tip of its nose. If the two horses like each other, they nibble each other along the top of the neck. If they don't, there may be a fight.

How do horses communicate with each other?

They make a number of different sounds. A *snort* is a danger signal. A *neigh* is a call that means "Hello, I'm here." A *whinny* means that the horse is excited about something.

Horses also communicate by movements. If their ears are laid back, it means they are angry or fearful. If they lash their tails back and forth, they are about to kick. When they stamp and prance, or dance sideways, they are excited and nervous.

How does a horse protect itself?

A horse usually runs away from danger. But if it is cornered, it will kick and bite.

Did horses always live on the earth?

No. There were no horses at all on the earth long ago. There were also no people, no cats, no dogs, no cows, and no elephants.

About 150 million years ago there were lots of water animals. But there was only one kind of animal that could live on dry land all of the time. It was called a *reptile*.

A reptile is cold-blooded, breathes air, and it can lay eggs with shells that can hatch on dry land. The dinosaurs were a kind of reptile. The land and waters of the earth were full of dinosaurs at this time. Some of them were meat eaters.

But then after a long time, a new kind of animal appeared. It was called a *mammal*. It was different from the dinosaurs and other reptiles. It had hair or fur and was warm-blooded. A young mammal grew inside its mother's body and was born alive. Then it was fed with its mother's milk. The milk came through special glands called *mammary glands*. The young ones sucked this milk until they were able to eat other food.

Was the horse one of these early mammals?

No. The horse came much later. At first the mammals were small and there were not many of them. The meat-eating dinosaurs ate them when they could.

But the dinosaurs died out about 70 million years ago. Then there began to be more and more mammals and many different kinds of them.

One kind of these mammals that lived on the earth 60 million years ago was the ancestor of the horse. It is called Eohippus (**ee-o-hip-pus**). It lived in the Eocene (**ee-o-seen**) period that lasted for 20 million years.

Did Eohippus look like a horse?

It looked more like a dog than a horse. It was about as big as a fox. But it was not a meat eater like a fox or a dog. Instead it "browsed." That means it ate leaves, berries, and fruits in the forest. We know this because its teeth were good for biting and crushing soft plants.

Eohippus horses had four toes on each front foot. They had three toes on each back foot. All the toes ended in separate small hoofs. The middle toe was larger than the side toes. The neck was short and thick.

When Eohippus horses were feeding, they had to watch out for danger. When they saw a beast with sharp teeth coming after them, they ran away if they could.

What happened after Eohippus?

During the millions of years since Eohippus, many, many horses have lived and died. Those that had longer legs and could run faster escaped from their enemies. The ones with shorter legs could not escape.

So the longer-legged, taller horses lived longer. They had more babies than the others. Their babies grew up and the ones with the longest legs who could run the fastest lived longest and had more babies.

One of the ways that the horse's legs became longer is that horses came to stand on the tip of the middle toe. (Try standing on tiptoe and see how much taller it makes you.)

Gradually more and more horses were tall, long-legged, and stood on their middle toes.

Eohippus lived on the plants in the forest, and for millions of years the horses that came after Eohippus did, too.

But about 25 million years ago the climate changed from warm and moist to colder and drier. Before the change there were forests, wet meadows, and swampy marshland. Now there were great plains of grass. Some horses who lived on these plains had bigger and stronger teeth than others. The teeth were longer and had hard ridges that could grind up tough grasses.

These horses lived the longest and had more babies than the ones that could not feed on grass.

So, gradually horses became grazers — grass eaters — rather than browsers that munched on leaves and fruits.

After sixty million years, horses were no longer small animals that lived in the forest. They were tall, long-legged, one-toed animals that chewed grass on the open plains.

How do we know about these horses of long ago?

We know about them because thousands of their bones and teeth have been found. Usually these bones are turned to stones. They are called fossils.

Where were these fossils found?

Some fossils were found in Europe, Asia, and Africa. But most of them were found east of the Rocky Mountains in the United States.

When the early horses lived there millions of years ago, this land was wet and marshy. When horses died, they often sank into soft mud along lakes and rivers. They were buried under the sand and mud and water. Slowly, the minerals from the water entered the bones and turned them to stone.

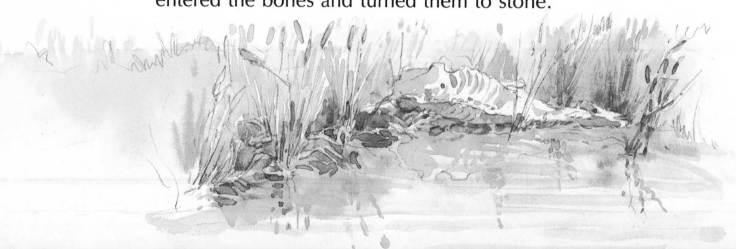

How are the fossils found?

Scientists who work in museums and universities go where the ground is bare and look for pieces of bones and teeth. They walk along the bottom of bare cliffs and slopes. They look for pieces of bones and teeth that are uncovered or might have fallen from the slope above.

When they find a bone, they climb up to a place where there might be many bones. If they are very lucky, they find the skeleton or head of some animal. Perhaps they find the skeleton of an early horse!

Sometimes farmers or travelers discover bones by accident and then they tell museums where the bones are.

When did people first use horses?

Cave men of the Stone Age used horses. But they did not use them to ride. They used them as food. In one camp in France, the broken and chewed bones of 100,000 horses were found. The camp was 25,000 years old.

Later, horses were used to pull carts or chariots. Horse bones were found buried in graves in Central Asia along with chariot wheels and human skeletons. The graves were 5,000 years old. The horses were important in war. People could fight from the chariots pulled by horses.

A long time after this, other men began to tame wild horses to ride them. For hundreds of years many battles were fought by men riding on horses.

Did Native Americans always ride horses?

No. Horses disappeared on this continent about 10,000 years ago. No one knows why. When the Spanish explorers came to North America in the sixteenth century, more than 400 years ago, American Indians saw their first horses. Later when the Spanish set up cattle ranches in the Southwest the Indians were able to get horses for themselves. They soon became great horsemen.

Are horses used much today?

Horses are still used on ranches to round up cattle for branding and vaccinating. But most farmers use tractors instead of horses for work on the farm. And we now use automobiles, railroads, and airplanes to travel.

People still enjoy riding horses. And they go to racetracks to watch horses race. Also, many horses are used in circuses, rodeos, horse shows, and in such sports as polo.

The author wishes to thank Mr. Morris F. Skinner, Frick Associate Curator, The American Museum of Natural History, New York, for reading the text of this book.

Thanks also to Mr. John Wolfson of the Claremont Riding Academy, in New York City, for answering many questions.

For Myron who loves the horses

ISBN 0-590-48448-6

Book design by Laurie Williams

Text copyright © 1973 by Millicent E. Selsam.
Illustrations copyright © 1995 by Scholastic Inc.

12 11 10 9 8 7 6 5 4 3 2   5 6 7 8 9/9 0/0

Printed in the U.S.A.   08

First Scholastic printing, April 1995